WORLD WAR I
AT SEA

A view of dreadnought *SMS Helgoland*, launched in Kiel 1909, ceded to Britain 1920, scrapped at Morecambe early 1920s. The picture shows one of its state of the art starboard 305mm heavy guns, some 150mm secondary guns and command bridge.

AS SEEN ON CONTEMPORARY POSTCARDS

NICK MILLER

Publisher: CreateSpace Independent Publishing Platform
Printer: CreateSpace Independent Publishing Platform
Copyright ©Nick Miller 2018
ISBN 10 1717 494838
ISBN 13 078 1717 494832

Price: £7.99

Front cover: It could be a send-off to sea in any country, any age. This is on a German card. The black, white red of the second German empire flutters as friends and relatives bid God speed, safe return.

The First World War at Sea

We think of the First World War as the great land war. And it was. But many of the roots of the conflict, especially as far as Britain was concerned, lay not in land might and European ethnic and territorial disputes, but in economic, industrial competition centred on the seas, on the threat to Britain's trade routes and colonial markets, and challenges to Britain's self-appointed role as global policeman and ruler of the waves.

Germany was the major European land power. However, it lagged centuries behind other European countries in the grab for colonies which could supply cheap labour and imports, and serve as a market for home products. Kaiser (Emperor) Wilhelm II came to power in 1888. He enjoyed land domination, but espoused wider ambitions. Germany wanted 'a place in the sun', colonies in Africa and Asia, like their European neighbours. Wilhelm supported the theories of USA naval strategist Alfred Mahan. He maintained that the secret to superpower status was a synthesis of commercial and industrial power with command of the sea. Thus in 1898 Wilhelm declared Germany's 'future lay on the water'. Germany commenced a massive naval expansion programme. A threat to naval supremacy unleashed alarm in the British Admiralty, Whitehall and Westminster. The arms race of the day became a naval one.

Britain had a policy of maintaining a fleet size twice that of potential adversaries – the 'Two Power Standard'. German expansion forced a rethink of this and the whole basis of British naval strategy. At the same time von Tirpitz, Secretary of State in the Imperial Naval Office, realised Germany may never match Britain in absolute ship numbers, and with a lack of naval bases worldwide could not compete globally. He argued, though, that harbouring a fleet capable of inflicting if not outright victory, then at the least decisive harm on Britain would oblige it to concentrate its fleets to face off Germany in home waters. This would tie down resources and restrain Britain from all-out attack for fear of fatal weakening of maritime domination and exposing the British mainland to invasion. Tirpitz also reasoned that parity with Britain could gradually be effected by selective encounters with sections of the British Grand Fleet, whereby German training, technological prowess and temporary numerical superiority could deliver a series of ever more crippling blows against Britain.

The arms race diverted huge budgets in both countries to shipbuilding and technology, in Germany even extending to deepening and widening the Kiel Canal between the Baltic and North Sea to accommodate the bigger ships. The lust was not just for more ships, but faster ones, better armoured, with more rapid and potent firepower over ever longer ranges. A step-change arrived with the launch of *HMS Dreadnought* in 1906. The British Orion class and later Queen Elizabeth class super-dreadnoughts presented even greater displacement and new 343mm then 381mm calibre cannons, firing near 900Kg shells up to 30Km.

New range finding and firing control apparatus that compensated for the rapidly varying pitch, yaw and roll of the ship raised gunnery accuracy. This and propellant improvements and heavier shells with greater penetration brought the precision firing of salvos from around 2Km range in 1900 to around 10Km by 1918 (full range was nearer 30Km for British guns, somewhat shorter for German ones).

Those decades also saw seeds of strategy transformations that would characterise 20th century war at sea –large scale mining; submarine lone raiders and packs, submarine reconnaissance and shields preceding sweeps by surface attackers; shipborne air capability; convoy formations; small group strikes rather than whole fleet set pieces. Radar surveillance and a still primitive sonar capability were about to transform naval warfare forever.

When war finally arrived an expectation was a prominent role of naval warfare, of a showdown between Britain's Grand Fleet and Germany's Hochseeflotte (High Seas Fleet) that would decide the outcome of the war. In the event it seemed like the whole naval affair went off as a damp squib. With the exception of the Battle of the Skagerrak/Jutland in 1916 there were not even any large scale confrontations.

This view misses the nature of war at sea. There are no areas of ocean to occupy and hold like one might on land, no key ridges to defend, no inching forward the territory controlled. The strategies of both Germany and Britain saw a playing out of von Tirpitz's risk fleet strategy and Britain's response to this. British naval theorist Julian Corbett realised another power may not want the prospect of a major showdown, but seek to gradually whittle down British supremacy. His counter to this was to employ blockades: close ones, such as mining of base approaches; and more distant ones: patrols to head off breakouts from base, shutting off access to the North Atlantic and English Channel to hem the Hochseeflotte into the North Sea and strangle German overseas trade.

The U-Boot campaign and blockades were as much a war of attrition as in the trenches and a significant factor in how the war ran and ended. Whilst one cannot dismiss the entry of USA in December 1917 as a factor in turning the tide in the land war, whether this made a fundamental difference to the outcome overall remains a topic of debate. Also potent forces in the endgame were Germany's disruption to Britain's supply routes, loss of merchant vessels and a replacement ship-building programme struggling to keep pace with losses. The consequence was an inability to 'keep the home fires burning' and economic privations that ever threatened to boil over into social and political discord. The British blockade fomented a similar situation in Germany.

As regards WW1 at sea, the early conflict saw actions in the Indian Ocean, Pacific and South Atlantic. Small German colonies in the Pacific and Indian Oceans were picked off by mid-1915. Hostilities persisted somewhat longer in German East Africa, involving armed motor boat exchanges on Lake Tanganyika.

Confrontations between Russian and Ottoman forces and some German vessels occurred in the Black Sea but had little influence on the European theatre. In the Mediterranean the Austro-Hungarian fleet was more or less confined to base by the blockade of the Adriatic. Some submarine warfare threatened movements in the Mediterranean, and the British navy, along with the land forces, suffered in Winston Churchill's ill-conceived disaster in the Dardanelles/Gallipoli.

The Germans cornered the Russian fleet into a largely defensive role in the Baltic. With the loss of the battle of Moon Sound (Oct-Nov 1917) Russia was removed from the maritime equation. Germany supported counterrevolutionary White forces in Finland and Russia until Britain and France took over that role in 1918.

Aside from U-Boot activity the one (in)famous naval event to the west was the shelling of Dublin from the Liffey on 26-27.4.16. The main focus from 1914 to 1918 remained the North Sea. Bases in the Orkneys (anchorage for the Grand Fleet, at Scapa Flow) and the Harwich Force curtailed German excursions into the Atlantic and English Channel. Along with ships positioned at different times in the Firths and East Coast ports these bases were launching points for sweeps of the North Sea to intercept German sorties.

Hochseeflotte ships bombarded east coast towns. There was a planned but aborted U-Boot, Zeppelin and cruiser operation against Sunderland. Encounters between sections of the Grand Fleet and Hochseeflotte took place in two battles of Helgoland – on 28.8.14 (von Tirpitz's son

Wolfgang was amongst prisoners rescued from SMS (Seiner Majestät Schiff, His Majesty's Ship) *Mainz* by *HMS Lurcher*) and a less consequential duel on 17.11.17. There were two battles of Dogger Bank. - on 24.1.15 and a skirmish on 10.2.16. The last largescale action of the war was the bungled raid on Zeebrugge and Oostende on 23.4.18.

The one major meeting of the two fleets, where in Churchill's words Admiral Jellico (British commander) could win or lose the war in an afternoon, took place on 31 May-1 June 1916 in the Skagerrak off the coast of Jutland. This was simultaneously the largest naval battle of all times -150 ships of the Grand Fleet ranged against 99 ships of the Hochseeflotte. It was also the last of its kind before developments immanent at Jutland/Skagerrak altered naval warfare for ever.

The Germans planned to provoke Beatty's large scouting squadron to put to sea to counter raids on shipping and lure them onto the full Hochseeflotte. This worked in as far as Hipper's scouting squadron engaged and badly mauled Beatty as planned, drawing him south to the full fleet. Unbeknownst to Hipper German radio messages had been intercepted and he pursued north only to find himself and the following Hochseeflotte facing the entire Grand Fleet.

Sixty miles away on the Danish coast the ensuing bombardments were heard as thunder. The Hochseeflotte might have been annihilated after Jellico manoeuvred his ships into crossing the T of the German line –where the full power of the whole British force could bear down on the German fleet, the latter able to reply only with their leading ships. Masterly counter-manoeuvres by German commander Scheer not only assured survival but in the resulting night battle in which the British and German lines crossed through each other in X formation, German night training meant the Grand Fleet losses were again appreciable.

Who won the battle provokes endless debate. Britain lost more ships, tonnage and men; Germany proved it could take on and bloody the whole Grand Fleet. The Hochseeflotte though never ventured forth again and resources were diverted to the U-Boot campaign.

A final combined submarine, air and entire Hochseeflotte sortie was ordered to inflict a major blow against the Grand Fleet and bolster Germany's hand in any peace negotiations. This senseless mission, as it was perceived, sparked mutiny in the Kaiserliche Marine (Imperial Navy). It rapidly spread to German ports and cities, beginning a political struggle between left and right eventually culminating in Hitler's Nazi party gaining power in 1933.

The U-Boot campaign and naval blockades were undoubted factors in the outcome of the war. The naval chapter of WW1 also confirmed Britain's decline and eclipse as the leading naval power. It spelled the end of Britain's world policing and colonial expansion activities. It opened new directions in strategy and technology that would shape sea warfare right through the 20th century.

The following pages present postcards and some other photographic documents that illustrate the actions and propaganda of the era, many of them not previously published. In 1914-18 there was no TV footage to inform the public of events, regular cinema newsreels were still a way off. There was no facebook or twitter and newspapers were not accessible to or read by all. Postcards, though, were a powerful medium of communication at that time. They spread news and portrayed to people back home the happenings on the front line – either as privately produced cards or via officially sanctioned images that presented a sanitised or biased view of events. And of course the messages and words between the lines on the back often painted a far more powerful picture than photographs ever could.

The Kaiser's uncle, Edward VII, arrives to launch *HMS Dreadnought* 10.2.06. Steam-turbine engines, ten 305mm/12 inch guns made it far faster, and delivered two and a half times the firepower of the next best battleship. Japan had started an all 'big gun' battleship earlier but failure of Armstrong's in Newcastle to supply the guns meant it was not realised. The race to for ever more powerful ships meant by 1923 *HMS Dreadnought* was obsolete and scrapped.

'Weser' works, Bremen. Boilers for *SMS Gneisenau*, launched 1906, powered by coal-fired triple expansion engines, top speed 23.6 knots. Sunk in the Falklands battle 8.12.14. The decades 1898-1918 saw introduction of smaller (more room for weapons) higher performance turbine engines (faster). More energy efficient oil fired propulsion extended geographical range and also diminished smoke emissions that easily disclosed ships' positions in pre-radar days.

Gun turrets under construction, Armstrong-Whitworth Elswick works, Newcastle on Tyne. They built warships for Britain, Italy, Brazil, Chile, Argentina, Ottoman Empire, and others, and a dozen cruisers for Japan. Once the German East Asia fleet was defeated Japan exploited the opportunity to occupy German territories in the Pacific and expand influence in China. In 1917 they sent a force to the Mediterranean to support anti U-Boot activity.

Salvo from the 305mm/12 inch, 50 calibre guns of a German Derfflinger class ship. From 1898-1918 calibre of standard naval 'big guns' practically doubled. Propellant advances meant ever heavier shells were projected over ever further ranges. By the end of the war 900Kg shells could reach nearly 20 miles. The illustration also shows the considerable hindrance to range finding that smoke from one's own guns could pose. The insets illustrate the size of shells in relation to a child and to a grown man.

"IT'S A LONG WAY TO TIPPERARY!"   17

To cope with ever increasing gun sizes the Midland Railway introduced special rolling stock in 1911 capable of transporting ordnance with a gross weight in excess of 100 tons. This 380mm/15 inch diameter 16 meter/52.5ft long naval gun leaving Foleshill Works, Coventry, in 1915 was used to fire 879Kg shells up to almost 20 miles at a muzzle velocity of over 1600 mph.

Stapellauf
S. M. S. „Kaiserin".
11. 11. 11.
11 Uhr 11 Min. vorm.
Verlag Phot. Karl Koch.

SMS Kaiserin (Empress) launched at 11.11 a.m. on 11.11.11. A fateful date, no one foretelling that on 11.11.18 it would all end ignominiously in dark, damp French woods. In many ways emblematic of the fate of the German navy, *Kaiserin* was launched in splendour by royalty. It participated in several actions, including the Skagerrak/ Jutland battle 1916, but its full potential was never exploited. After it was scuttled in Scapa Flow in 1919 it lay 23 fathoms down before raising in May 1936 to be towed to Rosyth for scrap.

Крейсеръ I ранга „Олегъ". (6675 тоннъ)   Изданіе Н. Апостоли. 132

Another ship of its time. Russian cruiser *Oleg*, launched St Petersburg 1903 for the Baltic fleet; reinforced 2nd Pacific fleet in Japanese-Russian war 1905. Interned in Manila. Returned to Baltic. When war broke out it went on mining duties and actions against German commerce and military at Bornholm, Gotland and Åland. In the 1917 Revolution the crew supported the Bolsheviks. It was torpedoed and sunk 17.6.19 at Kronstadt by British speedboat *CMB-4* which was supporting counter-revolutionary White Forces.

British fleet firing a salute to the Kaiser, June 1914. Pre-war contact between cousins George V, Wilhelm II and Tsar Nikolai II and their navies was extensive. Kiel Week, pictured here, was one regular meeting. Amongst the pomp and banquets, there was always intensive espionage. In 1914, key targets were range finding and firing control apparatus, torpedo launchers, radio rooms. Admiral Warrender's parting radio message to all ships just 6 weeks before the war: 'Friends in past and friends for ever'. The insets show cousins Kaiser and Tsar, and Edward VII with nephew Kaiser Wilhelm.

AGRAHAMS. 789   H.M.S. "ENGADINE" SEAPLANE CARRIER (CAMOUFLAGED).   DEVONPORT

The first seaplane attack was 6.9.14 Japan's *Wakamiya*, attacked Austria's *Kaiserin Elisabeth* in Shandong. The converted cross-channel ferry *HMS Engadine* (picture), took part in the first ship launched British air raid, 25.12.14, on the port of Cuxhaven. The first ship-launched aerial torpedo attack came from *HMS Ben-my-Chree* in the Dardanelles 12.8.15. Initially planes were winched in and out the water. On ship take-off and landing emerged only at the end of the war.

On 2.8.14 *SMS Augsburg* and *Magdeburg* mined and shelled Libau (now Liepāja, Latvia), the first shots in the war with Russia. Many German naval paintings were by Willy Stöwer (1864-1931), a favourite of the Kaiser (including his famous picture in *Die Gartenlaube* of the *Titanic* sinking). His postcard reproductions of paintings were generally sold to support sailors' families and the Deutscher Flottenverein (German Fleet Association) of which he was a board member.

On 26.8.14 Light cruiser *Magdeburg* ran aground in fog off Odensholm (Gulf of Finland), whilst minelaying. Torpedo boat *V26*'s endeavor to tow her off and attempted scuttle were frustrated by Russian cruisers *Bogatyr* and *Pallada*, which partially wrecked *Magdeburg*. The significance of the incident was the recovery of three intact cipher books. One came to Britain, to Room 40, the Admiralty's crypto-analysis department and was to exercise a crucial impact on the naval war.

The first German-British surface naval confrontation of the war, 28.8.14. Tyrwhitt's Harwich Force, with 1st Battle Cruiser Squadron reinforcements, attacked known German patrols off Helgoland. Tyrwhitt was soon outgunned by *SMS Frauenlob, Köln* and *Stettin* and shore batteries. The Cruiser Squadron moved in, sinking *SMS Ariadne, Köln* and *Mainz*. The British flattered to deceive. British strength in numbers hid problems with communication and organisation which would loom large in later years. The German experience was instrumental in them shifting to mines to protect their approaches rather than ship patrols.

A jolt to morale came on 22.9.14. Kapitänleutnant Weddingen in *U9* spotted cruisers attached to the Harwich force in the Broad Fourteens (south Dogger). *U9* sank *HMS Aboukir, Hogue* and *Cressy*, taking 1450 lives. It taught Germany the potential of the U-Boot and Britain its threat. *U9* also sank *HMS Hawke* off Aberdeen 15.10.14. Weddingen died on 18.3.15 when *U29* attacked *HMS Neptune* in Pentland Firth but was cut in two by *HMS Dreadnought*. Inset is a portrait of Weddingen and his wife.

Both sides armed commercial vessels. Cunard liner *RMS Carmania* of the Liverpool - New York route and *Cap Trafalgar* of the Hamburg-Süd Amerika line became armed merchant cruisers. The liners met on 14.9.14 off the Ilhas da Trindade, 20°S 29°W, off the Brazilian coast (card caption is wrong, it's not Trinidad). After two hours *Carmania* was ablaze and almost sunk. *Cap Trafalgar* in a similar state did sink. The encounter was the first in which two liners fought each other.

Madras/Chennai, India 22.9.14. *SMS Emden* destroying oil tanks and merchantman. It is said that 'Amdan' became Sinhala and Tamil slang for 'crafty', 'ruffian', which Emden was. As a lone raider in SE Asia, disguised as *HMS Yarmouth,* it captured over 20 ships; sank Russian cruiser *Zhemchug* and French destroyer *Mousquet* in Penang. *HMAS Sydney* disabled *Emden* when it attacked British installations on the Keeling/Cocos Islands, 9.11.14. Kapitänleutnant Mücke and his shore party escaped the Australians by commandeering schooner *Ayesha*, and making the hazardous thousands of miles trip back to Germany, to be welcomed back heroes of the day.

Fregattenkapitän v. Müller

Karl Müller (1873-1923) commander of *SMS Emden was* noted for his chivalry, strict adherence to the law, desire to avoid loss of life, and returning civilians to neutral ports. He was imprisoned on Malta and later at Sutton Bonnington (Notts) where he led a tunnel escape.

In peacetime he was elected a conservative MP in the Freistaat Braunschweig parliament (Free State of Brunswick in the Weimar Republic). He died from complications of malaria contracted whilst in the tropics. Unlike many contemporaries he wrote no memoirs, declaring he would 'not be able to escape the feeling I was coining money from the blood of my comrades.'

The Sinking of H.M.S. "Audacious" in the Irish Sea, by a German Mine, during the Great War - 1914.

Super-dreadnought *HMS Audacious* 27.10.14 struck a mine laid by converted liner *Berlin* off Lough Swilly, Ireland. All hands were saved by White Star liner *SS Olympic, HMS Liverpool, HMS Fury* and others (a sailor on *Liverpool* died from debris when *Audacious* exploded). The event highlighted design problems in British ships with compartmentalisation. The loss was ordered to be kept secret and *Audacious* appeared on fleet lists till 1918, but passengers on *Olympic* published photos like this one on their arrival in the USA.

Vernichtung der englischen Panzerkreuzer „Monmouth" und „Good Hope" an der Küste von Chile (Santa Maria) durch die deutschen Panzerkreuzer „Scharnhorst", „Gneisenau" und „Leipzig".

The Admiralty was shocked out of its delusion of invincibility when on 1.11.14 Maximillian von Spee's East Asia Squadron defeated the British South Atlantic Squadron under Sir Christopher Cradock off the coast of Chile at the battle of Coronel. Cradock perished with all hands when *HMS Good Hope* was sunk. This was the first defeat of the royal navy in over a century. Coronel was avenged at the battle of the Falklands just over a month later, 8.12.14.

"INVINCIBLE". (FLAGSHIP)   "CANOPUS".   "CARNARVON".   "INFLEXIBLE".

"CORNWALL".   THE FOUR SUNKEN GERMAN WARSHIPS.   "KENT."

"BRISTOL".   ADMIRAL GRAF VON SPEE   VICE ADMIRAL SIR F.D.S. STURDEE.   "GLASGOW."

THE FALKLAND ISLANDS BATTLE. THE GERMAN NAVY PAID QUICKLY FOR OUR LOSS OF THE GOOD HOPE & MONMOUTH. ON D. 8 THE SCHARNHORST (1) LEIPZIG (2) NÜRNBERG (3) & GNEISENAU (4) WERE SIGHTED OFF THE FALKLANDS BY A BRITISH SQUADRON UNDER VICE ADMIRAL SIR F STURDEE. AN ACTION FOLLOWED & THE FOUR GERMAN SHIPS WERE SUNK.

In December 1914 at the Falklands Admiral Sturdee, with eight cruisers, all more powerful than von Spee's, sank *SMS Gneisenau, Scharnhorst, Leipzig* and *Nürnberg*. Post-war British intelligence revelations suggest von Spee was tricked into thinking no British strike force was around after receiving fake German messages, made possible by the capture of German codes. Von Spee and his sons perished that day. The admiral's intention had been to proceed to the Río de la Plata to refuel. In one of those strange twists of fate the battleship named after him, *Graf Spee*, was scuttled there twenty-five years later almost to the day, on 17.12.39, to avoid sinking by the awaiting *HMS Achilles, Ajax* and *Cumberland*.

SMS Dresden escaped, but was eventually run down off Chile, again possibly cornered because of decoded radio intercepts. With scarcely any coal and engines worn out after 16000 miles at sea, it was scuttled off the Juan Fernandez Islands 14.3.15, with the crew interned in Chile for the duration of the war. This marked the end of the German East Asia Squadron and any concerted naval activity outside European waters. However, armed merchantmen and liners did continue some activity on the high seas.

One such armed freighter was *SMS Möwe*. In Jan 1916 it captured *SS Appam* en route from Senegal-Plymouth. *Möwe* brought *Appam* to Virginia to sell the $3-4 million booty (including gold bullion and a leopard named Pompey). The British owners sued for possession, their right upheld by a federal judge. The German government appealed. A landmark Supreme Court ruling declared foreign belligerents could not violate USA neutrality by bringing ships to their ports under such circumstances.

"Appam" (engl. Dampfer)

Torpedoes were in production 50 years before WW1, gradually improving in propellants, range, charge, direction control and launch methods. Fast, easily manoeuvrable torpedo boats posed a threat to cumbersome battleships and a swarm attack could break up entire battle formations. Britain favoured the torpedo destroyer, combining torpedo capability with heavier armament. Germany built over 300 lighter, faster torpedo boats. On the left the 9th Torpedo Flotilla is steaming towards Helgoland, 1915. Right is *HMS Lance* a torpedo destroyer assigned to the 3rd destroyer flotilla at Harwich. On 5 Aug 1914, less than 24 hours after war was declared *Lance* fired the first shots of the war at sea – to challenge converted steamer *SMS Königin Luise* laying mines off the Thames estuary.

The Sinking Of The German Warship, "Bleucher" © I.F.S. From N. Moser, N.Y.

On 24.1.15 the British surprised German ships at Dogger Bank, from decoded messages about their sortie. *SMS Blücher* was hit by around 70 shells and 7 torpedoes, losing 792 men. Beatty's crippled flagship *HMS Lion* was towed back with a shield of 50 ships. *SMS Seydlitz* nearly foundered from flawed magazine design and poor ammunition handling procedures, factors present too in British ships. The Germans corrected these, the British did not - to their later cost at the battle of Jutland/ Skagerrak.

John Bull in Angsten

Mit Zeppelin und U —
Jagt man mich immerzu
Zu aller Hohn und Spotte! —
Ich bin in größten Nöten,
Mein Anseh'n ging schon flöten
Durch diese Luxusflotte!

Both sides taunted each other about not daring to send out their fleets. This card by celebrated Leipzig postcard artist Arthur Thiele (1860-1936), better known for his anthropomorphic cats and seaside humour, parodies a German verse to describe John Bull running scared in the face of the Zeppelin and U-Boot attacks. The card below comments on the outcome of the battle of Jutland/ Skagerrak 1916 where British propaganda acknowledged some damage to the Royal Navy whilst claiming much deeper wounds inflicted on the German fleet.

IF THEY'D ONLY LET HIM OUT !

The British bulldog against the German Dachshund was a popular image. Reg Carter (1886-1949), Southwold postcard artist (and early illustrator for Beano comic and Ladybird books) drew seaside and social commentary comic cards. Here *HMS Itard* (Hit Hard!) waits for the German fleet to be let out. The Kiel canal linked the German Baltic ports with North Sea bases, saving a lengthy and exposed trip round the north of Denmark. The inset is a British card issued after the battle of Jutland/ Skagerrak claiming a British advantage – I got some but you should see the other chap.

Another parody, this time of Goethe's 1780 poem Wanderers Nachtlied (The wanderer's song of the night), as familiar to German readers as Wordsworth's 'I wandered lonely as a cloud' was to British readers. The English Captain's Song: Below all the waves there's a U-Boot; scarcely a breath of Britain's fleet...Wait a while, soon you will be sinking too.

Lied des englischen Kapitäns.
(Frei nach Goethe.)

Unter allen Waſſern iſt — „U"!
Von Englands Flotte ſpüreſt du
Kaum einen Hauch . . .
Mein Schiff verſank, daß es knallte —
Warte nur, balde
Verſinkſt du auch!

Neat pun. Around 235000 mines were laid. These were partly defensively around ports and coasts, partly offensively in shipping lanes, to hem U-Boot activity. They were laid outside bases to catch exiting vessels. One such mine sank *HMS Hampshire* off Orkney 5.6.16, which was carrying Field Marshall Lord Kitchener on a diplomatic mission to Russia. It hit a mine laid on 28-29.5.16 by *U75* intended to sink Grand Fleet ships leaving for the battle of Jutland.

SO 'S MINE !

On 16.12.14 *SMS Derfflinger, von der Tann* and *Kolberg* shelled Scarborough, with its radio stations, Whitby with its coast-guard station. Major back-up waited in Dogger to confront expected reaction, part of the plan to whittle down the Grand Fleet. In Scarborough 18 died, 3 in Whitby (some sources say 7). A blow to British morale, the raid fuelled recruitment and propaganda - 'Remember Scarborough'- and was used to influence opinion in neutral countries.

SMS Blücher, Moltke, and *Seydlitz* attacked industrial, railway and port targets in the Hartlepools. Seven soldiers, 86 civilians and 8 Germans perished. Aside from loss of life and homes, and the Baptist church (picture), the raids highlighted the value of the captured German codes in predicting their movements, the Kaiser's over-cautiousness in not wanting to commit his fleet and flaws in British communications and organisation. These flaws led both navies to miss prime opportunities that day to strike significant blows.

BOMBARDMENT of LOWESTOFT ... KENT R.
SHELL WENT THROUGH 13 HOUSES ...
NOBODY KILLED ... INJURED MANY ...
12 ... SHELL WEIGHED 8 ... 90 ...

FLIGHT OF SHELL THROUGH MIDDLE OF HOUSES

On 25.4.16 a raiding party bombarded Lowestoft (minelaying base) and Yarmouth (submarine base), aiming to entice out and pick off elements of the Harwich Force and Grand Fleet. Inhabitants of Kent Rd had a miraculous escape when a 450Kg shell travelled through 13 houses without detonating. The raid drew a blank in terms of depleting the British navy. But also, despite warning of the raid via radio intercepts the British failed to drive home their advantage.

The Royal Navy was used not just for attacking Germany and its allies. They attacked the Irish too. The Easter Rising commenced in Dublin on 24.4.16. Troops attacking the Rebels lacked artillery. Dept of Agriculture and Technical Instruction boat *HMYacht Helga* had a fixed 12 pounder (sources conflict on calibre) and detachable smaller gun. The latter was remounted on a lorry by Sherwood Foresters on 27.4.16, but to little effect.

Die Englische Kriegsflagge!

In Nov 1914 Britain declared the North Sea a war zone, ships of any nation entered at their own risk. On 4.2.15 in response to this and the suspicion that British ships failed to fly a flag or sailed under false flags of neutral nations, Germany announced unrestricted submarine warfare on ships in British and Irish waters – adding that due to misuse of neutral flags 'it may not always be possible to prevent attacks on enemy ships from harming neutral ships'. The postcard caption: The English flag of war.

England's plight. U-Boot action sank around 5000 ships (3722 in the peak year 1917), almost 13 million tons. The map details sinkings Feb 1917-Jan 1918. Bottom left cites Winston Churchill's statement that land forces were lacking shells and detonators for want of ships. The emergency shipbuilding programme could not keep pace with losses. German High Command had believed that despite the danger of the USA entering the war if their boats were harmed, unrestricted U-Boot warfare could bring GB to its knees in 6 months.

Engl. Schiffbrüchige werden durch deutschen U-Kreuzer geborgen.

636.
F. Finke,
Wilhelmshaven

Real costs came in lives not tonnes. 15000 mercantile seamen perished. The image shows a U-Boot picking up survivors. The inset is a message 17.5.17 from John Nuttall on collier *SS Porthkerry*, to Mary in Newcastle Emlyn, little knowing the 'letter to follow' never would. En route from Cardiff to Sheerness *Porthkerry* went, against Admiralty orders, to aid crew from *SS Tycho*, torpedoed by *U40*, but was also torpedoed. John was one of the 7 dead from *Porthkerry*.

Torpedierter engl. Zerstörer „Patridge."

554.
F. Finke,
Wilhelmshaven

Torpedoing of destroyer *HMS Partridge*. It and *HMS Pellew*, were launched in 1916 as part of the emergency war programme. In December 1017 they set off on a regular convoy from Lerwick to Bergen with four armed trawlers and six mainly Scandinavian registered merchantmen. Near midday on 12.12.17 they encountered torpedo boats *G101, G103, G104* and *V100* off the Norwegian coast. All but *Pellew* were sunk. Ninety-seven were reported killed. 24 survivors were picked up by the torpedo boats.

GERMAN SUBMARINE HASTINGS, 3.

U118 was launched 23.2.1918. It was involved in mine laying. It sank *SS Wellington* off Cape Villano and tanker *Arca* off Tory Island. After the Armistice it was assigned to France for scrap. It broke loose under tow 15.4.19 and beached at Hastings. An instant tourist attraction, £300 viewing fees went to the Mayor's Welcome Home Fund. Coastguards W Heard and W Moore who showed people round inside died, apparently from effects of chlorine gas inhalation from the leaking batteries. It was finally broken up in situ.

What are you doing there ?
We're playing at blockades—
and Willie's a U-boat!

The blockade of German ports by Britain and the U-Boot war were not distant abstract ideas to the general population. Apart from the great loss of life in the mercantile marine and royal navy and disruption to military supplies, civilians on both sides felt the effects. There were shortages of essential foodstuffs, coal and other materials. This led to rationing, serious price rises and black market dealing. In Germany especially it led later on to starvation too. Here a characteristic picture by Bamforth & Co. artist Douglas Tempest (1887-1954) captures a child's eye view of an earnest situation.

The German U-Boat "Deutschland." Largest Merchant Sub-Marine in the World and her

Commander Capt. Koenig, arriving in New London, Conn. Harbor, November 1st, 1916.

One way to evade the blockade involved cargo submarines. *Deutschland* was a merchant vessel built for Norddeutscher Lloyd, with 700 ton cargo capacity. It traded with still neutral USA, delivering dyes, medicines, gems, mail, and bringing back rubber, nickel, tin, silver. In 1917 it was requisitioned and armed as *U-Kreuzer* (Cruiser) *155*. Long-range U-Kreuzer were used to mine USA ports and attack shipping there. *U156* shelled Orleans, Massachusetts on 21.7.18.

To curb U-Boot activity 70 ships attacked German U-Boot bases at Zeebrugge and Oostende on 23.4.18. Landing troops were to eliminate shore batteries. Cruisers *HMS Iphigenia, Intrepid* and *Thetis*, filled with concrete, would be sunk to block entry and exit. The plan failed. *HMS Vindictive* could not land troops at agreed positions; intact shore batteries disabled *Vindictive* and prevented the blockships moving into place. There were 8 Victoria Crosses, but 200 deaths. Britain boasted victory, but U-Boot activity resumed in days. The image shows the entrance to the port after the raid.

The long awaited showdown between the main fleets came on 31.5.-1.6.16 in the battle of Jutland/ Skagerrak. In the first phase of engagement Beatty's superior 1st Battle Cruiser Squadron facing Hipper's 1st Scouting Group suffered the loss of *HMS Queen Mary* and *Indefatigable* (explosion right; *HMS New Zealand* left in the photo). With *HMS Lion* badly on fire Beatty uttered his famous remark to flag captain Chatfield: 'There seems to be something wrong with our bloody ships today.' Sailors of *New Zealand* who witnessed the explosion later each wrote sympathy letters to families of those lost from *Indefatigable*.

A Town Class cruiser, probably *HMS Birmingham, Nottingham* or *Southampton*, off Jutland 31.5.16. *Nottingham* had intervened in the coastal raids 16.12.14, fought at Dogger 23.1.15, but was torpedoed by *U52* on 19.8.16. Water spouts 80-100 m high from falling shells dwarfed ships. Large shells were visible leaving opponents' guns. Alongside bodies and debris from sunk ships, crews reported swathes of sea thick with dead and stunned fish from the exploding shells.

Kleine Kreuzer und Torpedoboote fahren zum Angriff in der Skagerakschlacht.

169

Apart from long range exchanges between capital ships there were closer encounters between the destroyer forces. Both sides deployed torpedo attacks to target enemy ships and break up battle formations. At Jutland/Skagerrak eight Grand Fleet destroyers were sunk with loss of 532 lives. The Hochseeflotte lost five torpedo boats with 229 lives.

Ostfriesland, Friedrich der Große u. III. Geschwader in der Skagerrackschlacht 31. 5. 16. abend 7 1⁄2 Uhr.

51. F.Finke, Wilhelmshaven

Battleship *SMS Ost-friesland*, on 31.6.16 (the photo more likely peacetime manoeuvres). It was launched in 1909. At the end of the war It was not interned but ceded to USA as part of war reparations. USA General Mitchell maintained battleships were vulnerable to aerial bombardment. In July 1921 *Ostfriesland* was towed off Virginia Capes and hit with bombs of various weights. It eventually succumbed to 900Kg drops. Mitchell declared this marked the demise of floating fortresses and the need to reform naval building. General Pershing and others disagreed. Come the Second World War Mitchell's position was vindicated, with an ever longer list on all sides of major ships that were victims of aerial strikes.

V.45 mit 500 Geretteten von S.M.S. Lützow in der Skagerrack-Schlacht. Boot war damit noch im Gefecht.

662.
F. Pinke,
Wilhelmshaven.

Vice-admiral Hipper's flagship *SMS Lützow* received 24 heaviest calibre hits. In the midst of battle he managed to board torpedo boat *G39* and transfer later, again under heavy fire, to *SMS Moltke*. At 02.20h over 1000 survivors boarded torpedo boats *G37, G38, G40* and *V45* (pictured with those rescued lining the decks). At 03.20h on 1.6.16 *V45* was involved in exchanges with *HMS Garland* and *Contest* and at 04.30h with cruiser *Champion* and destroyers *Moresby, Obdurate, Maenad* and *Marksman*, but without any losses.

*Panzerkreuzer „Seydlitz"
brennend während der Seeschlacht*

The previous page and the card below show *SMS Seydlitz* ablaze during the battle of Jutland/ Skagerrak, 31.5.16, with torpedo boats coming alongside to assist. At Dogger (1915) Germany saw the fatal flaw in design that permitted unstoppable spread of fire from the magazines and corrected this. Despite 32 direct hits and a torpedo strike from *HMS Petard Seydlitz* survived. The British had not corrected their design, a price paid dearly by *HMS Queen Mary, Indefatigable, Invincible, Defence, Warrior, Black Prince* and their 5140 dead at the battle of Jutland.

Light cruiser *HMS Chester* received 18 hits, wrecking all but one main gun. Jack Cornwell, a sight-setter on a 5.5"/139mm gun was badly injured, all comrades killed. Yet he stood by his station. *Chester* limped to Immingham. Cornwell died in Grimsby Hospital 2.6.16. A 16 year old Boy Scout doing his duty to the last was the hero Britain craved after Jutland. He received the VC, Victoria Cross. The insets are from a matchbox cover (left) and a collector card (right) from the 'Triumph' comic, 1927.

S.M.S. „Wiesbaden"

SMS Wiesbaden became immobilised, a sitting duck for the Grand Fleet. The sole survivor from the 475 crew was chief stoker Gustav Zenne (inset) who managed to hold onto drifting wreckage and was picked up by Norwegian steamer *Willy* from Drammen. In a book he recounted the inferno: 'skin yellow from the poisonous gases; gasping for breath; blinded by burning smoke; eardrums ripped, body racked by shockwaves from explosions. Charred comrades, bodies torn to shreds all around. Steel white hot from fires, lifeboats ablaze, those who leaped overboard killed by shrapnel raining down from the ship in a sea churned by salvo after salvo'.

Gorch Fock
geblieben in der Seeschlacht am Skagerrak
31. Mai — 1. Juni 1916

Poet Johann Kinau was one of the dead on *Wiesbaden*. His corpse later washed up on Väueröbod (Sweden), and he was buried on Stensholmen (the inset shows his gravestone) with five other Germans from the battle. A pen-name he used was Gorch Fock. In 1933 a training ship was named after him (now a museum ship in Stralsund). His work was tainted by the Nazis before restitution as a respected writer. In 1958 his brother Rudolf and niece Ulli launched the Bundesmarine (Federal Navy) windjammer *Gorch Fock*, still sailing today.

The Hochseeflotte practised manoeuvres intensively - torpedo boat breakouts, night fighting, the *Gefechtskehrtwendung* (illustrated), a 16 point/180° simultaneous, keel line turn. This was ordered by Admiral Scheer to masterly effect three times on 31.5.16: to counter Grand Fleet movements, extricate his fleet from murderous shelling when Jellico brought the entire Grand Fleet to bear on Scheer's line and then to disappear from under their noses into the encroaching night.

SMS Frauenlob was torpedoed by *HMS Southampton* in a fleeting but savage exchange between the German 4th Scouting Group and British 2nd Light Cruiser Squadron at practically point blank range soon after 22.00h, 31.5.16. From over 330 crew nine were rescued, one of whom died later. The image is a commemorative montage made on the 18th anniversary showing the eight survivors – Müller, Gerb, Siegrist, Marquardt, Hillenbrandt, Gunther(?), Barthold and Stolzmann.

Englische Flotte auf dem Rückmarsch nach der
Skagerakschlacht aus der Vogelschau.

152

Early morning 1.6.16. The Grand Fleet in a thirty mile wide formation to comb the area of the previous night and day's action in search of ships and survivors. The Germans picked up 77 British survivors, the British no Germans. The view is from Zeppelin *L11* (or possibly *L24*) which was sent out to ascertain British positions. Many ships loosed off shots, even 380mm shells, at the Zeppelin which retired well out of range.

Durchgehender Volltreffer auf Seydlitz
von der Back bis zur Proviantlast.

592.
f.Finke.
Wilhelmshaven

The force of explosions was tremendous. Shockwaves from the explosion that tore *Queen Mary* apart were so strong that below deck sailors on nearby ships believed they themselves had been torpedoed. Observers on *SMS Derfflinger* saw a 380mm shell hit *SMS von der Tann* that vibrated the ship along its whole length just like a tuning fork. Here the aftermath of elemental struggle from a direct hit on *SMS Seydlitz* – where the crew had fought for their lives in pitch black, air filled with nitrous and sulphurous fumes inducing fatal pulmonary oedema; furnace-like fire, superheated steam from fractured pipes. 98 died, 55 maimed for life.

„Derfflinger"
zerschossen nach der Seeschlacht.
31.5.1916. (Volltreffer +)

SMS Derfflinger June 1916 at Wilhelmshaven returning from Skagerrak/Jutland with 157 dead and 26 wounded. The + show some of the 26 hits received. It was late 1916 before *Derfflinger* and *Seydlitz* were ready for action again, though the rest of the surviving German ships were repaired by August. British repairs were largely completed by late July.

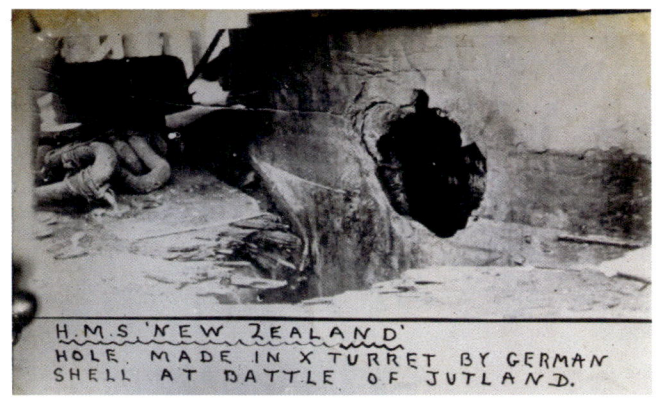

H.M.S 'NEW ZEALAND'
HOLE MADE IN X TURRET BY GERMAN
SHELL AT BATTLE OF JUTLAND.

At 16.00h on 31.5.16 Beatty's flagship *HMS Lion* was hit on Q turret (left photo) by a salvo from *SMS Lützow*. It blew off the roof, sending it flying around 150 meters into the air. *Lion* would have suffered the same fate as *Queen Mary* and the other battlecruisers that exploded that day but for Royal Marine Major Francis Harvey VC from Sydenham, Surry, who in his dying moments, both legs blown off, conveyed the order to flood Q turret to prevent the catastrophic spread of fire. *HMS New Zealand* (right) had a lucky escape at 16.26 when a 28 cm (11 inch) shell from *SMS von der Tann* pierced the barbette of its X turret, but only dislodged some armour, holed the deck and temporarily jammed rotation.

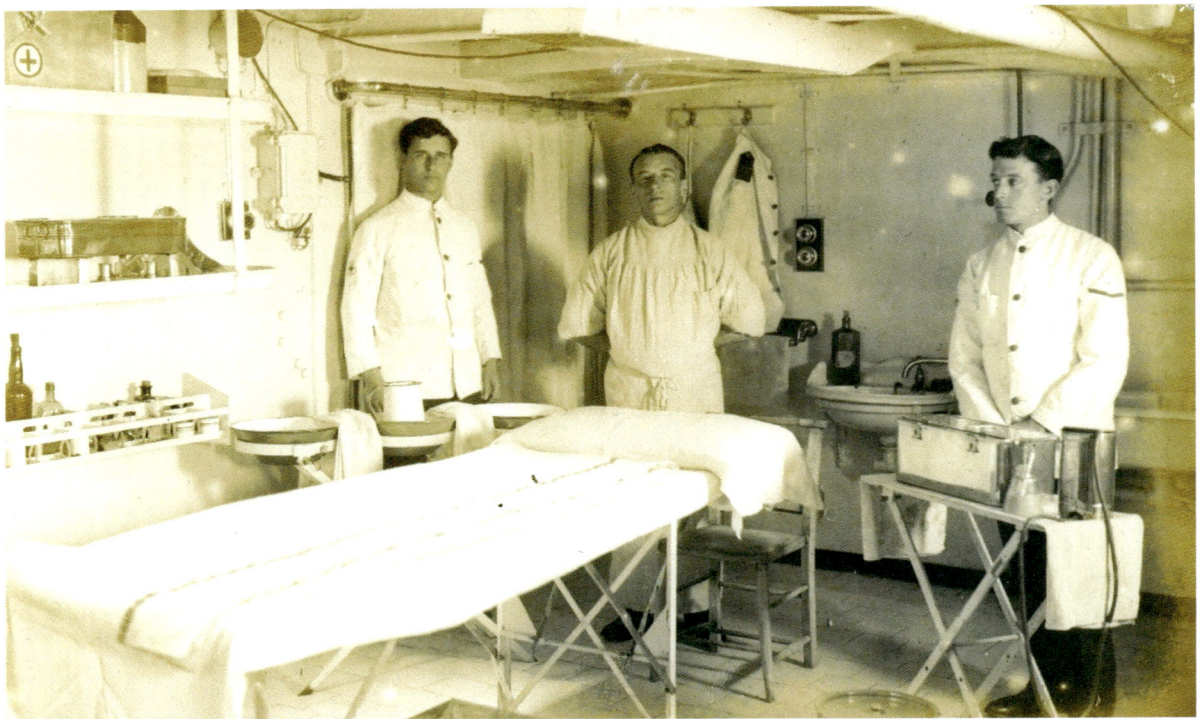

Hospital ships – mainly converted ferries and liners – treated and repatriated wounded to Britain or other bases. Britain had 26 in WW1, 12 were lost to mines and torpedoes. They were staffed by Medical Corps, Queen Alexandra's Royal Naval Nurses, Sick Berth Attendants and Stewards. Conscientious objectors also served on them. Some battleships had their own operating rooms – here on *HMS Barnham* – to treat lacerations, fractures, respiratory distress, burns and multiple trauma.

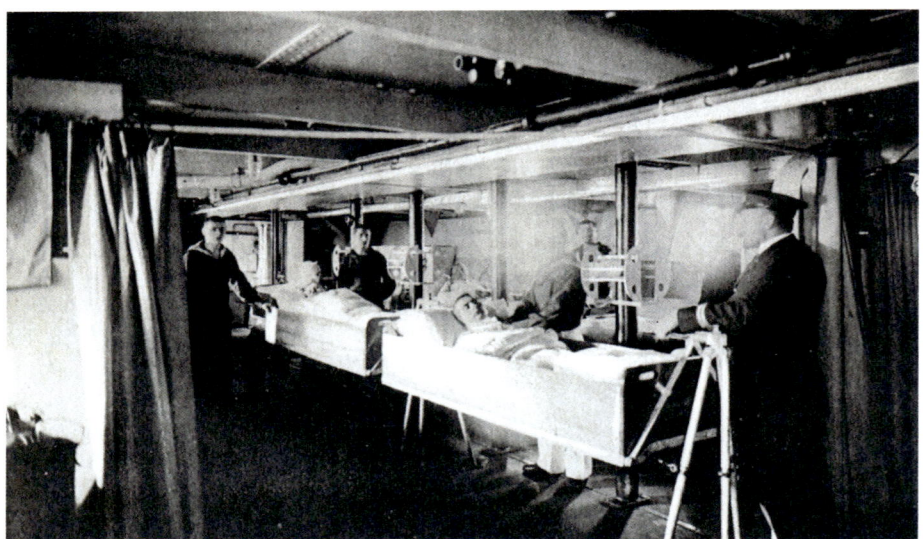

Sick bay on *SMS Yorck*. Magazine first aid kits had included picric acid for burns. Lessons from Jutland showed that this complicated not cured wounds. Treatments with aluminium acetate, boracic lint, and ointment of menthol, eucalyptus and carron oil, lime water combined with linseed oil, on exposed, not bandaged wounds became standard procedure. *Yorck* sank on 4.11.14 returning from a raid on Yarmouth and Gorleston. A navigational error in dense fog led it into one of its own German minefields.

U-Kreuzer.

101

Die sich weigernd in See zu gehende Mannschaft wird von U-Kreuzer und Zerstörer zur Kapitulation gezwungen.

German naval command planned a massive final operation starting on the Flanders coast and Thames, intending to draw out and engage the whole Grand Fleet. Unrest amongst crews was long rife, spurred by the Russian 1917 Revolution. When assembly orders were issued crews on several ships refused to cooperate in what was seen as a senseless, futile assault, sparking mutiny in other bases and shore garrisons and full scale revolution. Here *SMS Thüringen* and *Helgoland* which refused to sail lie under arrest by torpedo boats *B110, B112* and *U135* (the X, left) in Schillig Roads, off Wilhelmshaven, 30.10.18.

Burying the dead from the revolution in Kiel. Unrest spread around Germany with profound consequences. Revolutionary Sailors' and Workers' Councils sprang up, their slogan Frieden und Brot (Bread and Peace). By 7.11.18 King Ludwig II of Bavaria was forced to abdicate, followed by other German princes. On 9.11.18 Kaiser Wilhelm II himself abdicated (not till 28.11.18 officially) and a

Bestattung der Opfer der Revolution, Kiel, 10. November 1918.

republic was declared. Such was the atmosphere as the Armistice was signed on 11.11.18.

The last U-Boot action occurred two days before the Armistice, on 9 November 1918. In another of those ironic coincidences *U50*, under Heinrich Kukat sank *HMS Britannia* off Cape Trafalgar by the Straits of Gibraltar, a symbolic portent that Britannia's rule of the waves and the heady legacy of Trafalgar really were drawing to a close.

Barrages across the Dover Straits, deep mining the North Sea passage to the Atlantic and convoy formations were turning the U-Boot tide by 1918. 178 U-Boote were lost in the war. In 1918 at the end of the war the surface fleet was interned, but the U-Boot fleet had to surrender to Tyrwhitt, commander of the Harwich force, with no prospect of return. Some submarines were scuttled others incorporated into allied navies. Yet others were scrapped. Those ceded to Britain berthed at Harwich before dispersal to other ports.

On 16.11.18 Admiral Beatty read Konteradmiral Meurer and his staff the terms of their surrender on Home Fleet flagship *HMS Queen Elizabeth*. The agreement led to internment of the bulk of the German fleet by Britain. Other ships went later to France, USA, Japan. Before leaving their base at Wilhelmshaven they were fully disarmed and all instruments removed. The picture shows shells being removed from *SMS Friedrich der Große*.

Previous page: 21.11.18. Operation ZZ saw 70 German ships (4 joined later) escorted across the North Sea by nearly 200 battle ready British, Dominions and allied ships. They sailed to the Forth for removal of flags, then on 25-27.11.18 to Scapa Flow. The card shows crew of *HMS Queen Elizabeth*, with anti-flash masks ready for action even though the German fleet was disarmed. Masks and gauntlets only became standard after experiences of treating burns from the battle of Jutland.

The November Revolution instigated heated debate and activity. A further crescendo came with the communist inspired Spartacus uprising, January 1919. Sailors, soldiers and civilians manning a machine gun in Berlin. Karl Liebknecht and Rosa Luxemburg, founders of the German Communist Party and involved in leading the revolt were executed by the opposition with full complicity of the social democrat government.

Below, a Freikorps armoured car and flamethrower unit in Berlin. Chancellor Ebert's social democrat government gave free rein to the right wing Freikorps to suppress the Spartacists. Later left-wing moves were also brutally subjugated by the Freikorps with thousands murdered. In this atmosphere the Weimar republic was born. It set the scene for years of left-right struggle culminating in the Nazis' rise to power in 1933.

The sun setting, literally and metaphorically, on the Hochseeflotte in Scapa Flow. They were guarded first by the Battle Cruiser Force, later reduced to Squadron strength, with armed trawler and drifter patrols. The photo shows German destroyers/torpedo boats anchored in Gutter Sound, with capital ships north and west of Cava Island.

A former Norddeutscher Lloyd liner, most likely *Schleswig* (possibly *Sierra Ventana)*, later a hospital ship, then troop transporter bringing back Scapa Flow internees, spring 1919. Twenty thousand sailors arrived in Scapa Flow in November 1918. By that Christmas repatriation reduced the number remaining in Orkney to below 5000, later 1800. Crews received no shore leave, no visits to other ships, minimal rations and infrequent post.

A reason for reducing to skeleton crews was because many ships fell under control of revolutionary Sailors' Councils. British and German authorities feared unrest. Admiral Reuter also feared the imminent Treaty of Versailles would gift his fleet to Britain. On Midsummer Day 1919, with most British ships out on torpedo practice, he pre-emptively issued the order 'Paragraph 11. Bestätigen' - 'Paragraph 11. Acknowledge'. In contemporary slang 'Confirm Paragraph 11' meant 'continue boozing'. Here it was the agreed signal to scuttle all ships. The photo, taken at 15.50, gives a clear shot of *SMS Hindenburg* going down and crews from other ships being towed ashore at Flotta.

On learning of Reuter's orders Admiral Fremantle turned his ships immediately, radioing ahead to beach as many vessels as possible. Flagship *SMS Friedrich der Große* sank at 12.16h. At 15.50h British ships arrived to find German ships sunk or sinking. Fifty-two ships sank. Three cruisers, one other capital ship and 18 destroyers either remained afloat or were grounded. British boarding parties killed Korvettenkapitän Walther Schumann of *SMS Markgraf* and eight German sailors, their graves still in Lyness Cemetery on Hoy. Left is *SMS Hindenburg*; on the right are torpedo destroyers sinking or beached on Fara Island.

Crew from *SMS Nürnberg* being towed to *HMS Revenge*, allegedly being shot at despite raised hands.

It's 1936. Tugs Bertha, Metinda and a third prepare to tow away (most likely) *SMS Kaiserin*. In 1922 Stromness Salvage Syndicate bought a destroyer for breaking - amongst other things selling boiler tubes as curtain rods and coal to local merchants. From 1923-39 Cox & Danks and Metal Industries Ltd raised all but seven vessels by winching or by sealing them, pumping in air and towing away to scrap. From 1956 ex-diver Arthur Nundy's company and later Campbell and Co used explosives to blast and lift up remaining parts.

SMS Moltke provides an interesting afternoon outing at Rosyth in 1927. Recycled Hochseeflotte steel from *SMS Großer Kurfürst* was included in panels for the iconic liner *Queen Mary*. Post World War II metal that had been produced in pre-atomic bomb days, and was therefore minimally radioactive, fetched premium prices. The invaluable German steel was used in highly sensitive scientific and medical instruments. It even found its way into the *Voyager II* spacecraft.

Recycled materials may be one legacy of war, but human loss represents an irretrievable cost. Some seamen sank with their ships, some died of wounds ashore. Weeks and months after battles bodies were washed up on distant shores. Local children with sailors from pre-dreadnought battle-ship former *SMS Wittelsbach* lay a wreath at Skagen by the graves of British fallen from Jutland washed up on Denmark's north west coast. *Wittelsbach* (launched 1900) served as a depot ship for minesweepers from 1919-21 tasked with clearing sections of the North Sea. The picture comes from a sailor who had served on *Derfflinger*.

In memoriam cards mourned lost loved ones. Hermann Reiter, an engine driver's son from Mühlsdorf perished on *SMS Lützow*. Georg Grillenberger of Egersdorf sank at 02.10h, 01.6.16 with 843 comrades on pre-dreadnought *SMS Pommern*, after it was struck by one, maybe two torpedoes from *HMS Onslaught*. Herbert Rogers, son of Edward and Ellen from Trowbridge who lived with his wife on Gunner St, Portsmouth died on *HMS Tipperary* along with 150 others of its 197 crew. It also sank around 02.00h after a cataclysmic mauling by *SMS Westfalen* and *Nassau*. Suddenly exposed in their searchlights, in four minutes from 23.20 they fired 150 rounds of 5.9 inch shells at point blank range into *Tipperary*. The survivors abandoned ship and left it to sink.

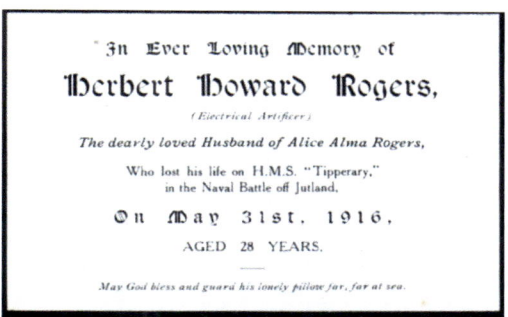

Burial at sea of Jutland Heroes
HMS Malaya

The postcard shows burial at sea on 1.6.16 of the remains of some of the 63 killed (two more died later of wounds) aboard *HMS Malaya*, during the battle of Jutland, their bodies sewn in sackcloth/ hammocks, feet weighted down with shells. The Inset shows the plaque from Malaya's chapel, for the 65 dead.

1933 marked the start of a period of ascendency for the fascist right following the sea-saw right-left political struggles sparked by the 1918 Sailors' Revolution. The card shows Hitler salutes at the 1936 Skagerrak commemoration. That year two more battleships would be laid down, soon to pick up where the Hochseeflotte left off. They were *Bismarck* and *Tirpitz* - named after the chancellor who forged the Second Reich and Grand Admiral Tirpitz, architect of Kaiser Wilhelm II's navy.

A Skagerrak-Jutland commemoration. Following the Treaty of Versailles Germany retained some obsolete pre-dreadnought cruisers. Ships in attendance here are probably former *SMS Hannover, Schlesien* and *Schleswig-Holstein*. By the mid 1930s they were being replaced in Hitler's Kriegsmarine by new ships with names like *Scharnhorst, Gneisenau, Lützow, Blücher, Hipper, Scheer* and *Graf Spee*. Echoes of 1914-18.

A painting by Hans Bohrdt (1857-1945), a self taught painter who succeeded in gaining the patronage of the Kaiser himself. His painting of 'The Last Man' became emblematic of loyalty to the flag to the last and was widely used at the time for propaganda purposes. The scene is the battle of the Falklands 8 December 1914 when outnumbered German ships fought the British. The back of the card has Heinrich Röser's poem of the same name inspired by the picture.

A typical sentimental card of the age. There's no U-Boot (not that we see anyway), but the image unconsciously captures other key new components of warfare that will alter naval encounters in the 20th century out of all recognition from the tactics and strategies of the past centuries. On the rigging the wires for radio and radar. In the air reconnaissance capability and aerial attack planes.

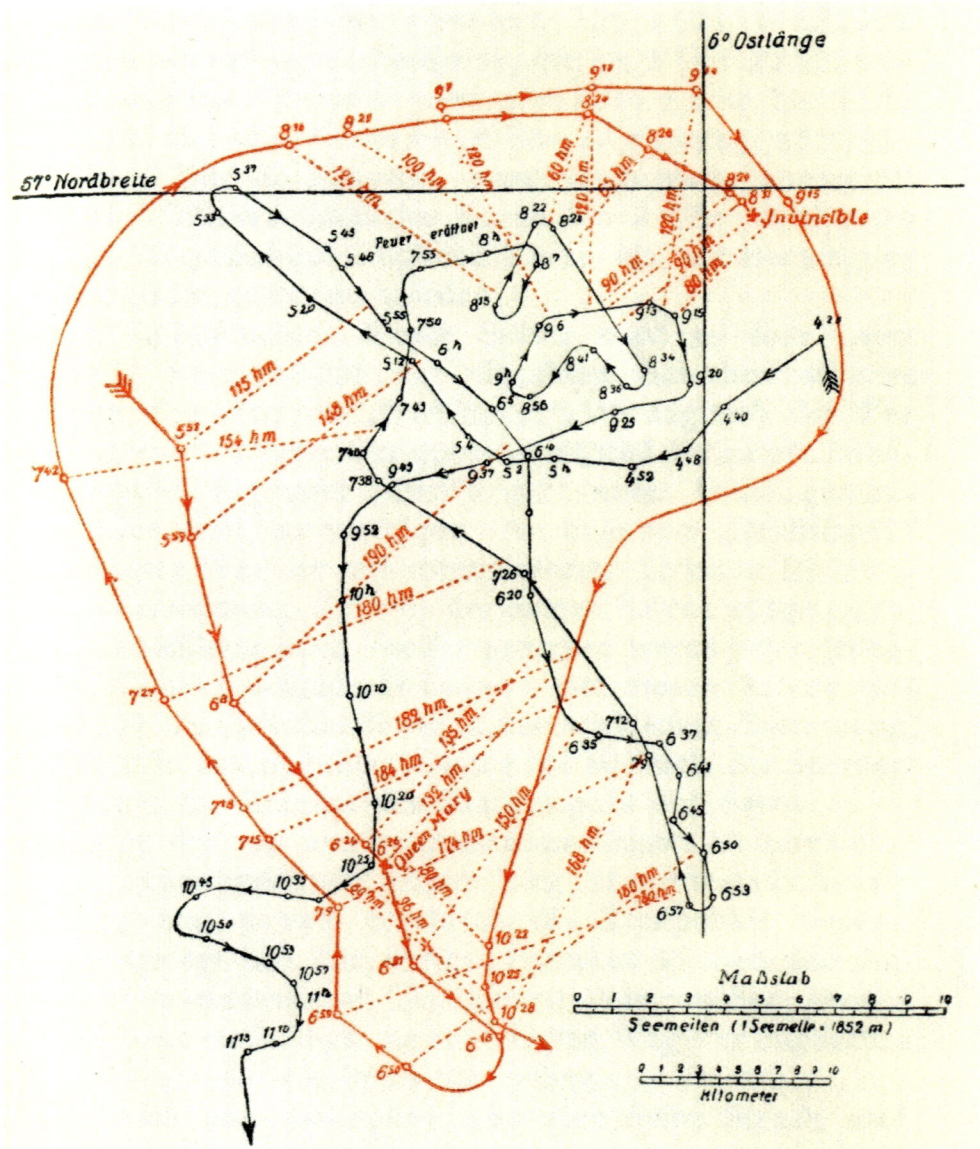

The black line traces the course of *SMS Derfflinger* during the battle of Jutland-Skagerrak. The three *Gefechtskehrtwendungen* are clear to see (top centre), as is the night course (bottom left) when the two fleets crossed paths. The red arrows show the course of British ships engaged by *Derfflinger* with the dotted lines giving the range and line of fire of exchanges.

Printed in Great Britain
by Amazon